BATTLES
OF THE CIVIL WAR

GAIL FAY

Heinemann Library
Chicago, Illinois

www.heinemannraintree.com
Visit our website to find out more information about Heinemann-Raintree books.

To order:
☎ Phone 888-454-2279
⌨ Visit www.heinemannraintree.com to browse our catalog and order online.

Edited by Megan Cotugno
Designed by Ryan Frieson
Illustrated by Mapping Specilaists, Ltd.
Picture research by Tracy Cummins
Originated by [select]
Printed in [select]

14 13 12 11 10
10 9 8 7 6 5 4 3 2 1

Library of Congress Cataloging-in-Publication Data
Fay, Gail.
    Battles of the Civil War / Gail Fay. — 1st ed.
       p. cm. — (Why we fought, the Civil War)
    Includes bibliographical references and index.
    ISBN 978-1-4329-3910-6 (hc)
    1. United States—History—Civil War,
1861-1865—Campaigns—Juvenile literature. I. Title.
    E470.F378 2011
    973.7'3—dc22
                         2009050008

Acknowledgments
The author and publishers are grateful to the following for permission to reproduce copyright material:

Corbis pp. 5 (© Louie Psihoyos/Science Faction), 35 (© Blue Lantern Studio); Library of Congress Prints and Photographs Division pp. 7 left, 9, 10, 12, 13, 14, 15, 16, 17, 20, 21, 22, 24, 25, 26, 27, 28, 30, 33, 36, 39, 40, 41, 42, 43; National Archives pp. 7 right, 31 (War and Conflict CD); The Art Archive pp. 11, 38 (Culver Pictures); The Bridgeman Art Library International p. 19 (Peter Newark Military Pictures).

Cover photo of Union troops fighting Confederates, January 15th, 1865 reproduced with permission from Library of Congress Prints and Photographs Division.

We would like to thank Dr. James I. Robertson, Jr. for his invaluable help in the preparation of this book.

Every effort has been made to contact copyright holders of any material reproduced in this book. Any omissions will be rectified in subsequent printings if notice is given to the publisher.

All the Internet addresses (URLs) given in this book were valid at the time of going to press. However, due to the dynamic nature of the Internet, some addresses may have changed, or sites may have changed or ceased to exist since publication. While the author and Publishers regret any inconvenience this may cause readers, no responsibility for any such changes can be accepted by either the author or the Publishers.

Contents

Why Did We Fight the Civil War? 4

Who Fired the First Shots? 8

What Was the First Major Battle? 10

Why Is the Battle of the Ironclads Important? 14

What Happened at the Battle of Shiloh? 17

Who Won the Second Battle of Bull Run? 20

What Was the Bloodiest Day of the War? 22

What Happened at the Battle of Fredericksburg? 26

What Happened at the Battle of Chancellorsville? 28

Which Battle Was Fought for Control of the Mississippi River? . 30

Which Battle Is Considered the Turning Point in the War? 34

Did Black Soldiers Fight in the Civil War? 38

What Happened During Sherman's March to the Sea? 40

How Did the Civil War End? 42

Timeline 44

Glossary 46

Find Out More 47

Index 48

Throughout this book, you will find green text boxes that contain facts and questions to help you interact with a primary source. Use these questions as a way to think more about where our historical information comes from.

Some words are shown in bold, **like this**. You can find out what they mean by looking in the glossary, on page 46.

Why Did We Fight the Civil War?

The Civil War is also known as the War Between the States. The war was fought over differences between northern states and southern states. There were three main differences.

Different Economies

By the mid-1800s, the North and South had developed different economies, or ways of making money. Most people who lived in the North had jobs in **manufacturing** and trading. They made things and sold them.

> "I believe this government cannot endure, permanently half *slave* and half *free*. . . It will become *all* one thing or *all* the other."
>
> —Abraham Lincoln, 1858

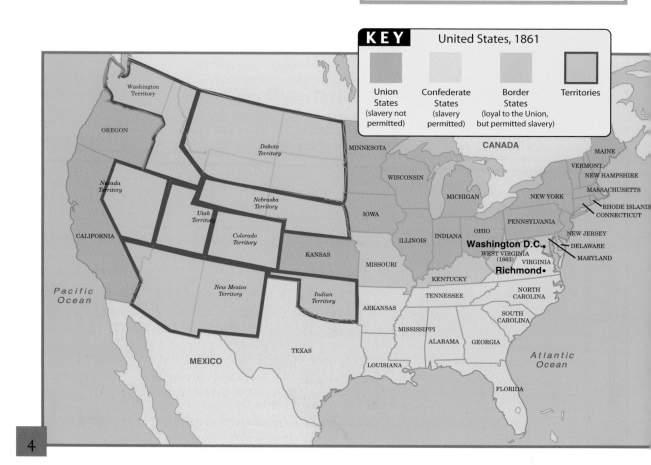

KEY United States, 1861

Union States (slavery not permitted)

Confederate States (slavery permitted)

Border States (loyal to the Union, but permitted slavery)

Territories

Most people in the South were farmers. Some people in the South owned **plantations** and grew crops such as tobacco and cotton. A plantation contained 100 or more slaves. In the South, about 125 landowners in each state possessed this wealth. Northerners did not need slave labor to run the factories.

Different Views on States' Rights

People in the North thought laws for the country should be created by the **federal**, or national, government. People in the South did not agree. They thought states should have the right to make their own laws, even if they were different from the federal laws. In particular, Southerners wanted to protect their right to own slaves.

Different Views on Slavery

In the mid-1800s, many Northerners joined the **abolitionist** movement. Abolitionists wanted to end slavery in the whole country, not just the North. Most Southerners did not agree. They felt slavery was essential to their farming way of life.

This is a photo of slaves working on a plantation on Edisto Island, South Carolina. About 125 landowners in each Southern state possessed enough wealth to own slaves.

The Last Straw

In 1860, Abraham Lincoln was elected president. Lincoln opposed slavery. Many Southerners felt the president would use his **federal** powers to force them to free their slaves. Rather than give up its southern way of life, South Carolina left the nation in December 1860. In early 1861, Mississippi, Florida, Alabama, Georgia, Louisiana, and Texas also **seceded**.

The seven states that left the Union became the Confederate States of America, also known as the Confederacy. Representatives from each Confederate state met in February 1861 and elected Jefferson Davis as their president. The Confederacy then chose Richmond, Virginia, as its capital.

President Lincoln and the Union leaders were willing to fight to keep the states united as one nation. Davis and the Confederate leaders were willing to fight for their rights.

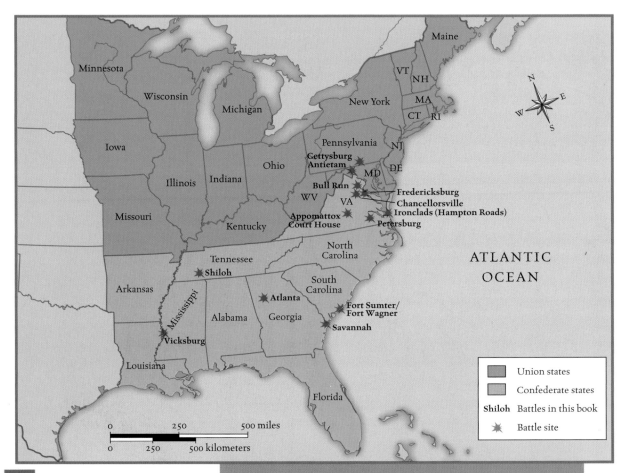

Did more battles take place on Union land or on Confederate land?

About the Battles

The Civil War lasted from April 1861 to April 1865. During that time, the North and South fought each other in more than 8,700 **engagements**, which resulted in more than 750,000 deaths (this number includes civilians). More people died in the Civil War than in any other war in U.S. history.

Some Civil War battles are known by more than one name. This is because the South named battles after the nearest city, while the North named battles after the nearest river or stream. Battles were fought in many states, but most took place on southern land.

This book covers 15 battles involving different armies from each side. The main army for the North was the Army of the Potomac. The main armies for the South were the Army of Northern Virginia and the Army of Tennessee.

Abraham Lincoln was president of the United States during the Civil War.

Jefferson Davis was president of the Confederacy.

Who Fired the First Shots?

After leaving the Union, South Carolina wanted to control all **federal** property within its borders. This included Fort Sumter, located in Charleston Harbor about 5 kilometers (3 miles) from the South Carolina shore. The U.S. Army had moved about 76 soldiers to the fort after South Carolina **seceded**.

On April 11, 1861, the Confederacy demanded that the federal troops leave the fort. The Union refused. At 4:30 a.m. on April 12, the Confederates fired on Fort Sumter from the shore **batteries**. The Union troops fired back, but they did not have as many soldiers or weapons as the Confederates. They were also running out of food. On April 13, the Union army **surrendered**, and on April 14 they left the fort. The South had won the first battle of the Civil War.

One Union soldier died during a gun salute as the American flag was being lowered in defeat, and two people were injured.

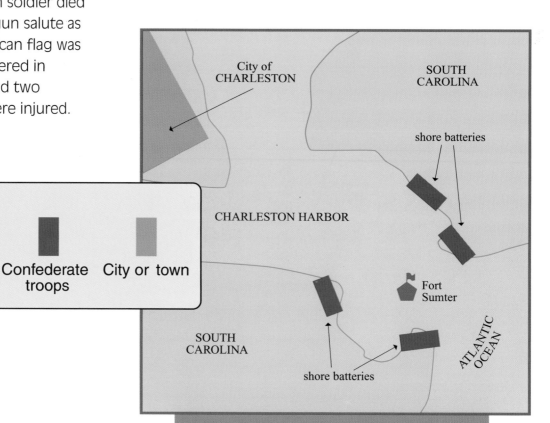

KEY

Union troops   Confederate troops   City or town

City of CHARLESTON

SOUTH CAROLINA

shore batteries

CHARLESTON HARBOR

Fort Sumter

SOUTH CAROLINA

ATLANTIC OCEAN

shore batteries

Fort Sumter was surrounded by powerful shore batteries that could easily hit the fort. The cannons the Yankees had in the fort were not as powerful.

After the battle at Fort Sumter, there were now 11 states in the Confederacy and 23 states in the Union. Jefferson Davis and President Lincoln both asked for volunteers to fight. In preparation for war, both sides made guns and ammunition. They also made uniforms—blue for the Union **Yankees** and gray for the Confederate **Rebels**.

BATTLE OF FORT SUMTER

Fort Sumter, South Carolina

April 12–14, 1861

One killed, two wounded

Confederate victory

WHAT WENT WRONG?

1. The North was outnumbered in manpower and gun power.
2. The North ran out of food and ammunition. The men had been there for four months, and a ship had been prevented from bringing them supplies.

Primary Source:
Fort Sumter, 1865

This is an interior view of Fort Sumter. The fort was named after Thomas Sumter, a Revolutionary War hero from South Carolina.

Thinking About the Source:

Look closely at the photo. Describe what you see.

What's missing from this image?

If this photo were taken today, what would be different?

What Was the First Major Battle?

After the loss at Fort Sumter, President Lincoln wanted to end the war and reunite the nation as quickly as possible. This was partly because he felt pressure from Northerners to stop the southern rebellion. In June 1861, General Irvin McDowell suggested a plan to invade the South near Manassas, Virginia. Instead of an army, McDowell had an armed mob that was nowhere near ready to fight. Pressures from the president and the public forced McDowell to take the offensive.

Why did McDowell choose Manassas? It was a small town with a big railroad junction. If the Union could take control of the railroad lines, they could prevent the **Rebels** from getting food, ammunition, and soldiers. It also meant the Union could use the railroad lines to transport their own supplies and troops.

This is an illustration of the Battle of Manassas (also called the first Battle of Bull Run). The North named this battle after a creek known as Bull Run. The South named it after the nearby town of Manassas.

The South also knew that the Manassas railroad junction was important. General Pierre G. T. Beauregard already had Confederate troops stationed there. He knew that the **Yankees** were going to attack, but he did not know when.

The Battle Begins

Beauregard had several spies in Washington, among them socialite Rose O'Neal Greenhow. Confederate scouts patrolled the Potomac River and kept the general informed of all movements. He also read the Washington newspaper daily to keep on top of events that were happening. When Beauregard heard of McDowell's plan, he moved 21,000 troops from Manassas to Bull Run. Now the North would have to cross the creek and get past the soldiers to reach the railroad junction.

On July 16–18, 1861, General McDowell moved 35,000 soldiers from Washington, DC, to Centreville, Virginia. Many Northerners followed the troops and came out on the day of the battle. They packed picnic baskets and blankets, as if they were going to watch a sporting event. However, the spectators were not ready for the horror that they saw. On July 21, the Union attacked. This started the First Battle of Bull Run, as the North called it. The South named it the First Battle of Manassas.

Primary Source:
Confederate Soldiers, 1861

These Confederate soldiers from Virginia were known as Richmond Grays. This photograph was taken in 1861, at the beginning of the Civil War.

Thinking About the Source:

What types of details do you notice about this photograph?

If this photo were taken today, would anything be different?

A Different Strategy

At first the Union soldiers pushed the Confederates back, and it seemed like they might win. Then Confederate General Thomas Jackson tried a different strategy. Instead of rushing into the fight, Jackson and his men stood still. They waited for the Union soldiers to come to them. Confederate General Barnard Bee said that Jackson and his troops stood there "like a stone wall." This is how Stonewall Jackson got his famous nickname.

Jackson's plan worked. His **brigade** slowed the Union advance until the remainder of General Joseph E. Johnston's troops arrived from Winchester. Because some of Johnston's men wore blue uniforms instead of the usual Confederate gray, they confused the Union soldiers. When the South made one final charge with the additional troops, the Union soldiers panicked and ran. In a state of chaos and confusion, the **Yankees** retreated back to Washington, DC.

General Thomas "Stonewall" Jackson earned his famous nickname during the First Battle of Bull Run.

In seven hours of fighting, almost 5,000 Confederate and Union soldiers were killed, wounded, or captured. Both sides learned that this war was not going to be easily won.

Deserting the Battle

Both sides were unprepared for war. When fighting broke out, men on both sides went into shock and ran in terror. In some cases, whole **regiments** deserted the battle. This was not uncommon in the battles of the Civil War. Terrified soldiers fled many battles. In fact, the panic of the Union soldiers at the end of the First Battle of Bull Run stood out above everything else that day.

FIRST BATTLE OF BULL RUN

Manassas, Virginia

July 21, 1861

Nearly 5,000 dead, wounded, or missing

Confederate victory

General Joseph Johnston and his Confederate troops arrived by railroad to help the South win the First Battle of Bull Run.

Why Is the Battle of the Ironclads Important?

At the start of the Civil War, the North tried to force the South to **surrender** by blocking its ports. With its ports blocked, the South could not ship cotton to England, and it could not ship supplies to Confederate troops.

In response, the Confederacy built an **ironclad** warship to see if it could defeat the Union's wooden ships. They converted the USS *Merrimack*, one of the **federal** ships left behind when the Union abandoned their shipyards in Norfolk, Virginia. The Confederates changed the top of the *Merrimack*, added iron plates to the **hull**, and attached a **ram** to the **bow** of the ship. Then they renamed the ship the CSS *Virginia*.

Ironclad ships like this one have iron-plated sides, which are much harder to pierce than wooden sides.

The CSS *Virginia* Attacks

On March 8, the CSS *Virginia* steamed from the James River into Hampton Roads, the huge harbor at Norfolk, Virginia. There, the *Virginia* rammed the USS *Cumberland*, which sank. Then, the *Virginia* went after the USS *Congress*. The *Congress* surrendered after its cannons could not pierce the iron sides of the *Virigina*. The *Virginia*'s crew decided to attack the final Union wooden ship in the morning.

BATTLE OF THE IRONCLADS (USS *MONITOR* VS. CSS *VIRGINIA*)

Hampton Roads, Virginia

March 9, 1862

No deaths, less than 20 wounded

Tie

Sailors in the U.S. Navy have a moment to rest on board the ironclad USS *Monitor*.

The USS *Monitor* and the CSS *Virginia* fought each other in Hampton Roads Harbor, Virginia. This was the first battle between ironclad ships, and it changed the future of naval warfare.

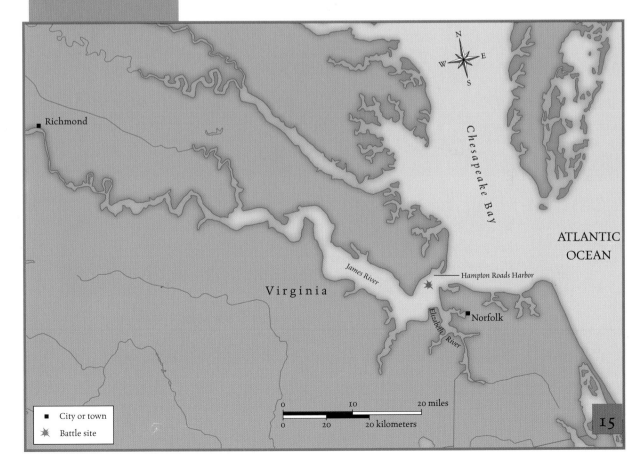

Richmond

Virginia

James River

Chesapeake Bay

ATLANTIC OCEAN

Hampton Roads Harbor

Elizabeth River

Norfolk

0   10   20 miles

0   20   20 kilometers

■ City or town

✹ Battle site

The *Virginia* Meets the *Monitor*

However, there was a surprise waiting for the *Virginia* when she steamed back into the harbor on March 9. The **Yankees** had their own **ironclad** called the *Monitor*. Before the *Virginia* could finish off the last wooden ship, the *Monitor* started firing. The two ironclads fought each other for about four hours. The *Virginia* was bigger and had more guns. The *Monitor* was faster and easier to steer. The *Monitor* also had a revolving turret with two cannons, so the captain did not have to turn the ship around to fire back. The ship could keep going straight, and the cannons could fire to the side or behind.

In the end, no one won the battle between the *Virginia* and the *Monitor*. Neither ship could puncture the other ship's iron plating. But naval warfare was changed forever that day. This battle marked the end of using wooden ships as fighting vessels.

The USS *Monitor*, in front, was faster and had a revolving turret. The CSS *Virginia* was bigger and had more guns.

What Happened at the Battle of Shiloh?

Both the North and South wanted to control **waterways** for the same reason they wanted to control railroads. Whoever was in control could stop the enemy from transporting supplies and troops. There are many rivers and streams between the Appalachian Mountains and the Mississippi River. And there were many battles in that area, too.

In early 1862, General Ulysses S. Grant and his Army of the Tennessee captured Fort Henry on the Tennessee River and Fort Donelson on the Cumberland River. Afterward, they moved south along the Tennessee River. Grant and his men established camp at Shiloh to await the arrival of a second Union army that was coming from Nashville.

BATTLE OF SHILOH

Pittsburg Landing, Tennessee

April 6–7, 1862

Nearly 24,000 dead, wounded, or missing

Union victory

General Ulysses S. Grant later became the 18th president of the United States.

Meanwhile, General Albert Sidney Johnston and his Confederate troops were heading north from Corinth, MIssissippi. Johnston wanted to attack Grant before the second Union **regiment** arrived. On the evening of April 5, Johnston's men moved into position. They waited in the dark.

April 6

The next morning, thousands of Confederate soldiers rushed into the Union camp. The Battle of Shiloh had begun.

Some of the **Yankees** set up a defensive line in a thicket (a dense growth of small trees). The fighting was very fierce in this area, which became known as the Hornet's Nest. The Confederates attacked the small Union line again and again. After six long hours, the Union troops **surrendered**.

April 7

Even though the Union soldiers surrendered at the Hornet's Nest, all was not lost. Because the men held on so long, Grant was able to gather troops in a different area to the north. Thousands of rested Union troops also had time to arrive. When the Confederates attacked this new Union line, they didn't last long. The **Rebels** were tired from their first day of fighting. They retreated by the end of the day, and the Yankees won the battle.

KEYS TO VICTORY

General Albert Sidney Johnston was one of the highest ranking generals in the Confederate army. His death on the first day of Shiloh was a major key to Union victory.

THE HORNET'S NEST

Every time the Rebels approached one part of the sunken road, the Yankees fired back with extreme intensity. As one Confederate soldier ran away, he yelled, "It's a hornet's nest in there!" That's how the Hornet's Nest got its name.

Above, Union troops defend against the Confederates in the Hornet's nest.

Who Won the Second Battle of Bull Run?

General John Pope and his Union soldiers controlled one of the bridge crossings at the upper Rappahannock River in northern Virginia. They were waiting for General George McClellan and his troops. Together they were going to attack the Confederates.

Confederate General Robert E. Lee knew that the **Yankees** had the advantage. They had a secure position and more troops on the way. His only hope was to attack General Pope before McClellan and his men arrived. So General Lee took a big risk and divided his army. Half went with Stonewall Jackson, and half went with General James Longstreet.

Jackson's men marched for two days and ended up behind Pope's troops. Just as Lee hoped, the Union soldiers turned around and went after Jackson. They could not wait for McClellan's **reinforcements** because it would endanger their position. On August 29, the Union attacked the Confederates and started the Second Battle of Bull Run.

"They [the Union soldiers] were so thick it was simply impossible to miss them."

—Confederate soldier at the Second Battle of Bull Run

General John Pope is possibly remembered most for his defeat at the Second Battle of Bull Run.

At the end of the first day of fighting, Pope thought the Union was winning. On the morning of August 30, Pope sent a message to Washington, DC, relating the previous day's fighting. Pope did not realize that the other half of Lee's army was on the way.

Longstreet and his 30,000 men arrived late on August 29, but waited until the afternoon of August 30 to launch their attack. Pope was not aware of Longstreet's presence until the attack came. The Confederates won again at Bull Run.

SECOND BATTLE OF BULL RUN

Manassas, Virginia

August 29–30, 1862

Approximately 25,000 dead, wounded, or missing

Confederate victory

General Robert E. Lee made a daring decision to divide his troops, and it worked. He led the Confederates to victory at the Second Battle of Bull Run.

What Was the Bloodiest Day of the War?

With their second victory at Bull Run, the **Rebels** regained control of most of Virginia. They also believed that Europe and the rest of the world would soon see the Confederacy as a separate nation. General Lee decided it was time to invade the North. Up to this point, all major battles had taken place on southern soil.

Primary Source: Robert E. Lee's Lost Order

One copy of Lee's plans was found by a Union soldier near Frederick, Maryland. The paper was folded in an envelope and wrapped around three cigars.

Thinking About the Source:

What, if any, words can you read?

What can you learn from examining this? (Hint: Think about how we communicate today.)

General Lee wrote up detailed plans for his attack. He was headed into Maryland. Lee divided his army as he had at Bull Run. He sent some to Harpers Ferry to capture the Union military post there. Others were sent farther north, with the goal of capturing the Baltimore and Ohio Railroad.

Before the Battle

On September 13, 1862, a Union soldier found one copy of Lee's orders. The plans told General George McClellan that Lee had divided his army. McClellan could have attacked the outnumbered Confederates. If he had done so, he might have destroyed Lee's Army of Northern Virginia and ended the war. But McClellan was cautious and waited.

Lee took a position at Sharpsburg, Maryland, on the west side of Antietam Creek. He waited for Stonewall Jackson to join him with the troops that were at Harpers Ferry. On September 15 and 16, General McClellan moved the Army of the Potomac into position across the creek.

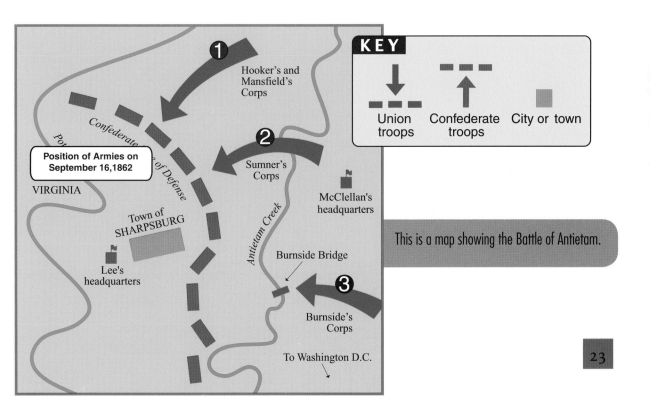

KEY

↓ Union troops

↑ Confederate troops

■ City or town

① Hooker's and Mansfield's Corps

② Sumner's Corps

McClellan's headquarters

Position of Armies on September 16, 1862

VIRGINIA

Confederate Line of Defense

Potomac

Town of SHARPSBURG

Antietam Creek

Lee's headquarters

Burnside Bridge

③ Burnside's Corps

To Washington D.C.

This is a map showing the Battle of Antietam.

The Bloodiest Day

The day long battle began at dawn. Union soldiers attacked the Confederates' left **flank** and were pushed back three times. Intense fighting then took place at the center of the Confederate line at a sunken road that was later named Bloody Lane.

General Ambrose Burnside then led a Union attack at a stone bridge on the Confederate's right flank. A small group of Confederate soldiers—perhaps only 400 men—held off 12,000 Union attackers for three hours. Finally, the **Rebels** retreated back to Sharpsburg. Burnside led his troops across the bridge, only to be stopped by Confederate soldiers coming from Harpers Ferry. The troops fought until sundown, when the Rebels finally retreated. McClellan did not follow the Confederates, and the Battle of Sharpsburg, as the South called it, ended. It was a major victory for the North, but at a huge price. It was the bloodiest day in U.S. history, with 23,300 dead or wounded in about 12 hours of fighting.

BATTLE OF ANTIETAM

Sharpsburg, Maryland

September 17, 1862

Over 23,000 dead, wounded, or missing

Union victory

Burnside Bridge was named after General Burnside, who led the charge here against the Confederates.

The Emancipation Proclamation

Five days after the battle, President Lincoln issued the **Emancipation Proclamation**. This first version granted freedom to slaves living in Confederate states if those states did not return to the Union by January 1, 1863. The second version, which was issued on January 1, 1863, was more specific and named the states where the proclamation applied. It did not free slaves in the border states of Kentucky, Maryland, Missouri, and Delaware. These states sided with the Union in the war, even though some people there still owned slaves. By the end of the Civil War, approximately 4 million slaves were freed.

The Emancipation Proclamation is one of the most important documents in our nation's history. At the time it was issued, it represented the **federal** government's official stand against slavery.

After the battle, President Lincoln met with General McClellan and other Union officers.

What Happened at the Battle of Fredericksburg?

After the Battle of Antietam, General Burnside replaced General McClellan as commander of the Army of the Potomac. In late November 1862, Burnside started moving his army south along the Rappahannock River. His plan was to cross the river and capture the city of Fredericksburg, Virginia, before General Lee could station his troops in the hills overlooking the city. After that, Burnside would have a clear path to the Confederate capital of Richmond.

In order to cross the Rappahannock, the Union needed **pontoons**. However, the pontoon bridges didn't arrive on time. They were a month late! While the **Yankees** waited, the **Rebels** prepared for battle. They dug **trenches** in the hillsides above the city. They put their **infantry** and **artillery** in the trenches to protect them from enemy fire. The Confederates also positioned **sharpshooters** in buildings in downtown Fredericksburg.

On December 11–12, the Yankees finished the pontoon bridges and entered Fredericksburg. They drove the Confederates out and destroyed the city. That night, Lee's men waited in their trenches in the surrounding hills.

WHAT WENT WRONG?

The supplies that the Yankees needed to build pontoon bridges were late. When the Union troops finally crossed the river, 78,000 Rebels were waiting to fight.

Pontoon bridges allowed troops and artillery to cross the river.

General Ambrose Burnside is pictured here (center). Burnside was famous for his bushy side whiskers, which became known as burnsides. Today, we call them sideburns.

BATTLE OF FREDERICKSBURG

Fredericksburg, Virginia

December 13, 1862

Nearly 18,000 dead, wounded, or missing

Confederate victory

On December 13, Union soldiers marched out of the city, across an open field, and toward the hillsides. However, the Confederates were too well protected. In one area, **brigades** of Union soldiers rushed toward Rebels who were protected by trenches behind a low stone wall. One after another, these brigades were gunned down by the hidden Confederate troops. In 14 attacks, not one Union soldier made it to within 69 meters (75 yards) of that stone wall.

Finally, the Union army retreated. Once again the outnumbered Rebels defeated the Yankees.

What Happened at the Battle of Chancellorsville?

How the South Won

After the Union lost at Fredericksburg, President Lincoln replaced Burnside with a new commander named Joseph Hooker. Almost immediately, Hooker started building up the Army of the Potomac. He also developed a plan to catch General Lee and the Army of Northern Virginia.

General Joseph Hooker is pictured here on his horse. Hooker had a plan to catch General Lee, but it ended in Union defeat.

Hooker's plan was to send one third of his army to attack Lee and his troops from the front while they were still at Fredericksburg. Hooker and the other two thirds of the Union soldiers would then move up the Rappahannock River to attack Lee's **flank** and rear, cutting the **Rebels** off from Richmond.

On May 1, Hooker marched his troops through a thick wooded area toward the Rebel line. Then, unexpectedly, the Confederates opened fire. The confused Union troops retreated back to Chancellorsville. Hooker got nervous and decided to wait. Meanwhile, Lee took action. He left 10,000 men to guard Fredericksburg and took the rest to chase Hooker. Then Lee split his forces again. He sent 26,000 with Stonewall Jackson to make a surprise attack.

> ## BATTLE OF CHANCELLORSVILLE
> Chancellorsville, Virginia
> May 1–6, 1863
> Over 30,000 dead, wounded, and missing
> Confederate victory

Jackson and his men marched 19 kilometers (12 miles) to get around Hooker's flank. Two hours before dusk on May 2, Stonewall Jackson's troops burst from the woods. Jackson succeeded in surprising the **Yankees**. Hooker's men retreated. The battle continued four more days and ended in a Confederate victory.

How the South Lost

Though they won the battle, the Rebels suffered a great loss as well. During the moonlit night of May 2, Confederate soldiers accidentally shot Stonewall Jackson and several of his **aides**. Jackson was hit three times, and his left arm had to be **amputated**. He was moved to a plantation building to recover, but he developed pneumonia. On May 10, Stonewall Jackson died. The southern military lost a great general, and the Confederacy as a whole lost some confidence.

> ## KEYS TO VICTORY
> General Lee divided his army—not once, but twice! This decision has been called one of the most daring moves in military history, and it helped Lee defeat an army twice the size of his own.

Which Battle Was Fought for Control of the Mississippi River?

The Confederates controlled Vicksburg, Mississippi, a town located on the east bank of the Mississippi River. They had powerful **artillery** on the **bluffs** overlooking a huge loop in the river. From there they could protect the town and control several miles of the Mississippi River. President Lincoln believed that capturing this city was a key to winning the war. As long as the Confederates controlled Vicksburg, they controlled this part of the river and could freely move men and supplies.

BATTLE OF VICKSBURG

Vicksburg, Mississippi

May 18–July 4, 1863

About 6,000 dead, wounded, or missing

Union victory

The Union tried to dig a canal as a way to travel down the Mississippi River outside the firing range of the Confederate artillery at Vicksburg. They never finished the canal.

November to March: Failed Attempts

In November 1862, General Grant marched his troops toward Vicksburg, but the Confederates stopped them. Grant and his men retreated. They camped north of the city.

From January to March 1863, the **Yankees** made several attempts to cross the river and attack Vicksburg. Each time the **Rebels** stopped them. Then Grant came up with a daring new plan. They would attack Vicksburg from the south and east instead of from the north.

April to June: Grant's New Plan

During the month of April, Grant and the Army of the Tennessee marched south on the west side of the Mississippi River. While the troops were traveling on foot, 12 Union **ironclads** steamed down the Mississippi. They blasted their way past the Confederate **batteries** at Vicksburg and met Grant and his men on April 30. Then the gunboats ferried Union troops across the Mississippi River. Once across, the Union soldiers were in enemy territory. They were cut off from all Union communication systems and supplies.

In the spring of 1863, General Ulysses S. Grant devised a plan to capture Vicksburg.

Over the next three weeks, Grant's army marched 290 kilometers (180 miles). They first headed toward Jackson, the capital of Mississippi. The **Yankees** captured the capital without major fighting. From Jackson, Grant headed west toward Vicksburg, which was the last Confederate stronghold on the Mississippi River. The army arrived on May 18 and surrounded the city.

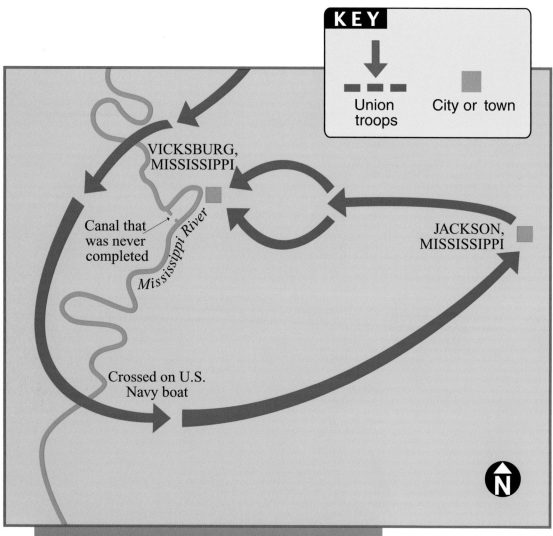

KEY

Union troops

City or town

VICKSBURG, MISSISSIPPI

Canal that was never completed

Mississippi River

JACKSON, MISSISSIPPI

Crossed on U.S. Navy boat

N

The Battle of Vicksburg was important because of the city's location on the Mississippi River.

From May until June, Grant's army bombarded Vicksburg. At the same time, U.S. gunboats attacked from the Mississippi River. The **siege** on Vicksburg lasted 48 days.

July: Confederates Surrender

On July 3, the Confederates finally raised the white flag in **surrender**. Grant and Confederate General John C. Pemberton agreed on the terms of surrender. Grant allowed Confederate soldiers to return to their homes instead of taking them all prisoner. On July 4, the **Rebels** officially surrendered the city of Vicksburg.

Although the Battle of Gettysburg (which is discussed in the next chapter) is more famous, the Battle of Vicksburg may have been just as important to the outcome of the war. By taking Vicksburg, the Union interrupted the flow of Confederate information, manpower, and supplies. The Mississippi River became the "highway" of the North instead of the South.

The siege of Vicksburg, headed by Union General Grant, lasted 48 days. Grant had help from the U.S. Navy in the capture of the city.

Which Battle Is Considered the Turning Point in the War?

In June 1863, General Lee and the Confederate Army of Northern Virginia marched into Union territory. There, they found much needed food and supplies, and then continued the northward march. The **Yankees** pursued them slowly and cautiously.

July 1: First Meeting

The Army of Northern Virginia and the Union Army of the Potomac met near the small town of Gettysburg, Pennsylvania. Around 5:30 a.m., Confederate soldiers went into town to find supplies. Instead, they ran into a full **brigade** of Union **cavalry**. The Confederates pushed the Union soldiers back into the hills. The **Rebels** won the first day.

The Confederates pushed the enemy back and won the first day of battle, but the Union started the second day with the advantage of higher ground.

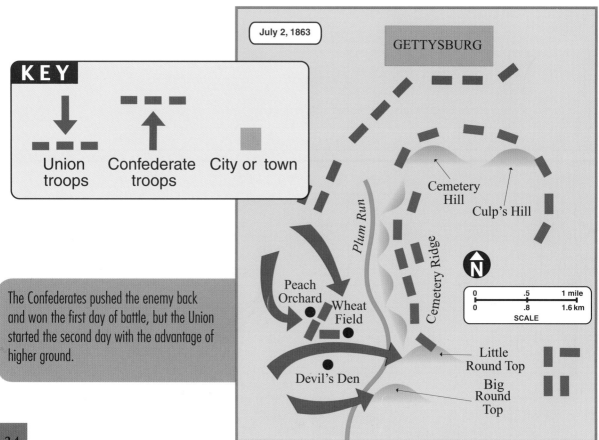

July 2, 1863

GETTYSBURG

KEY

Union troops
Confederate troops
City or town

Plum Run
Cemetery Hill
Culp's Hill
Cemetery Ridge
Peach Orchard
Wheat Field
Devil's Den
Little Round Top
Big Round Top

N

| 0 | .5 | 1 mile |
| 0 | .8 | 1.6 km |

SCALE

July 2: Main Fighting

When the second day of battle came, however, the Yankees had the advantage of higher ground. General George Meade stretched his Union troops across the top of Cemetery Ridge. The Rebels attacked the Union line at the south end of the ridge. The Yankees successfully stopped every Confederate charge. At the end of the second day, the Confederates were still at the base of the hill. The Union still controlled the higher ground.

> "The hoarse and indistinguishable orders of commanding officers, the screaming and bursting of shells, . . . the death screams of wounded animals, the groans of their human companions. . . It has never been [erased] from my memory, day or night."
>
> —Massachusetts private remembering the Battle of Gettysburg.

The Battle of Gettsyburg was an extremely bloody battle. Over 50,000 soldiers were killed, wounded, or declared missing.

July 3: Pickett's Charge

On the morning of the third day, Lee attacked the north end of the Union line. This attempt also failed. Then General George Pickett arrived with Confederate **reinforcements**. Lee decided on a massive assault in the center, which is now known as Pickett's Charge.

"Four score and seven years ago our fathers brought forth on this continent a new nation, conceived in Liberty, and dedicated to the proposition that all men are created equal."

—Abraham Lincoln, 1863
*from the **Gettysburg Address**. President Lincoln delivered this speech when part of the battlefield was dedicated as a cemetery.*

The Confederates first fired their cannons. The Union fired back. Soon about 250 guns on both sides were firing at once. The noise was deafening. Then the **Rebels** charged. Approximately 12,000 Confederate soldiers marched side by side across a half mile of open fields. Union soldiers just kept firing. There were so many Confederates marching toward them it was hard to miss. When the Confederate troops reached the edge of the clearing, they fought hand to hand with the **Yankees** using **bayonets**.

In Pickett's Charge, approximately 12,000 Confederate soldiers marched side by side toward the center of the Union line.

Though they fought hard, the Confederates were outnumbered. They finally had to withdraw. Fifty percent of the Rebels involved in Pickett's Charge were killed or wounded. The final retreat of Confederate forces took place on July 4.

The Battle of Gettysburg is the bloodiest battle in U.S. history. In three days of fighting, over 50,000 soldiers were killed, wounded, or declared missing. The combined losses at Vicksburg and Gettysburg devastated the South. The Rebels did not have resources to replace men or equipment.

More than 80,000 Union troops curved along Cemetery Ridge. Around 50,000 Confederate soldiers curved around the base of the hills.

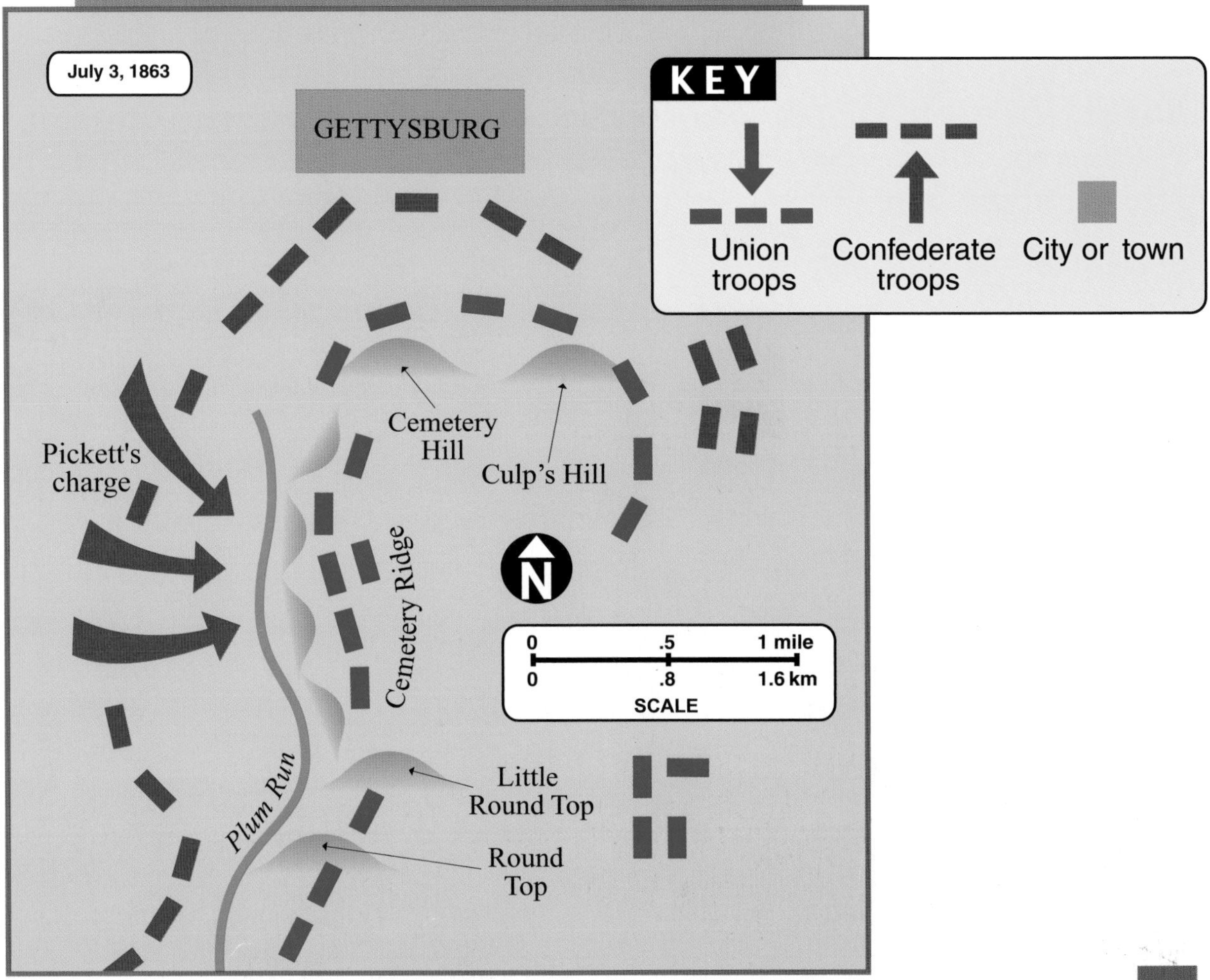

July 3, 1863

GETTYSBURG

KEY

Union troops   Confederate troops   City or town

Pickett's charge

Cemetery Hill

Culp's Hill

Cemetery Ridge

N

| 0 | .5 | 1 mile |
| 0 | .8 | 1.6 km |
SCALE

Plum Run

Little Round Top

Round Top

Did Black Soldiers Fight in the Civil War?

On January 1, 1863, the **Emancipation Proclamation** freed slaves in the **Rebel** states. Thousands of black people gained their freedom. The Union took advantage of this and recruited blacks into the army. By the end of the Civil War, nearly 200,000 black people fought for the North.

The most well-known black **regiment** is the 54th Massachusetts **Infantry**. The leader of this regiment was a white colonel named Robert Gould Shaw. Two men in the 54th were sons of Frederick Douglass, the famous **abolitionist**. Many people were **prejudiced** against blacks who gained their freedom. This was true in the military, too. Many doubted the men of the 54th Massachusetts could fight.

Colonel Robert Gould Shaw and his men charged over the walls of Fort Wagner.

Colonel Shaw was eager to prove the ability of his regiment. The 54th took part in the Union assault on Fort Wagner near Charleston, South Carolina. Most of the regiment made it over the fort's wall and engaged in hand-to-hand combat with the Rebels. Over one third of the 54th died, including Colonel Shaw. The Union lost this battle, but the men proved that they were brave and that they could fight. The 54th Massachusetts became the most famous black regiment of the Civil War because of its courage at Fort Wagner.

BATTLE OF FORT WAGNER

Fort Wagner, South Carolina

July 18, 1863

Nearly 2,000 dead, wounded, or missing

Confederate victory

Primary Source:
William H. Carney, ca. 1900

William H. Carney was the first black person to win the Congressional Medal of Honor in the Civil War. Carney won the medal for his bravery at the Battle of Fort Wagner.

Thinking About the Source:

What do you notice first about this image?

This picture was taken around 1900, decades after the Civil War ended.

Knowing this, what else do you think about the image?

What Happened During Sherman's March to the Sea?

In May of 1864, the Confederates only had two major armies left. General Grant wanted to keep them separated. He also wanted to destroy as much of the **Rebels'** war resources as possible. If he could accomplish both of these things, the war would end soon.

Grant ordered General William Sherman to move from Tennessee to Atlanta, Georgia, which was a major supply center for the South. Along the way, Sherman was to break up the Confederate armies under General Joseph Johnston. Sherman and Johnston fought each other off and on for two months. Sherman's army finally reached Atlanta in mid-July. They captured the city on September 2.

Since General Sherman ordered the troops to heat the railroad tracks and twist them around trees, these melted loops of metal were called Sherman's neckties.

On November 15, Sherman started his famous "march to the sea." The Union army burned the city of Atlanta when they abandoned it. As they marched, Sherman's men destroyed crops, property, and anything that might be of value to the Confederate army. After ripping up railroad tracks, the soldiers heated the metal rails and twisted them around trees.

The Union captured Savannah, Georgia, on December 21. But Sherman was not finished. After Sherman reached the sea, he traveled north into the Carolinas, leaving a similar path of destruction. In South Carolina, Sherman recaptured Fort Sumter, which had been lost at the beginning of the war.

General William T. Sherman tried to cause as much damage as possible to Rebel resources.

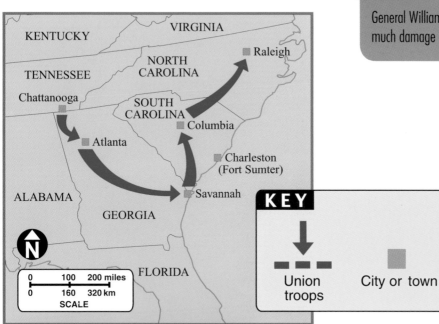

General Sherman's march began in Tennessee and ended in North Carolina.

How Did the Civil War End?

For six weeks, Grant fought his way southeast through Virginia. At the Battle of the Wilderness, Lee dealt the Union a tough loss, but Grant kept moving. Fighting then took place in Spotsylvania, where Grant's army was more successful. Lee then beat Grant to the North Anna River, where Confederates held the line against Union attacks.

The failed Union attack against Cold Harbor ended Grant's **Overland Campaign** to Richmond. During six weeks of fighting, the Union army lost over 60,000 soldiers. Grant finally decided to turn his attention to Petersburg. The struggle for Petersburg lasted almost ten months. Finally, on April 2, 1865, the **Yankees** captured the city. From there, Grant's troops marched to the Confederate capital of Richmond, which they found abandoned and burning.

These Union soldiers were photographed in the trenches during the **siege** of Petersburg, Virginia.

Lee's Surrender

The Yankees eventually chased the **Rebels** to the small town of Appomattox Court House, Virginia, and surrounded them. On April 9, 1865, General Lee **surrendered** to General Grant. The terms of the surrender stated that Confederate officers could keep their personal belongings, guns, and horses. Soldiers could keep their horses. They could also return to their homes. Though the war was over at this point, scattered fighting continued until the final surrender on May 26.

Just five days after General Lee surrendered, President Lincoln was shot at Ford's Theatre. He died the next day. It was a huge loss for both Northerners and Southerners. The reunited nation then moved on to rebuild itself in a period called the Reconstruction.

General Lee (right) signs the surrender papers while General Grant watches.

Timeline

November 6, 1860	Abraham Lincoln is elected president of the United States
December 20, 1860	South Carolina secedes from the Union
January–February, 1861	Mississippi, Florida, Alabama, Georgia, Louisiana, and Texas secede from the Union
February 9, 1861	Jefferson Davis is elected president of the Confederacy
April 12–14, 1861	Battle of Fort Sumter
April–May, 1861	Virginia, Arkansas, North Carolina, and Tennessee secede from the Union
July 21, 1861	First Battle of Bull Run
March 9, 1862	Battle of the Ironclads (USS *Monitor* vs. CSS *Virginia*)
April 6–7, 1862	Battle of Shiloh
August 29–30, 1862	Second Battle of Bull Run
September 17, 1862	Battle of Antietam
December 13, 1862	Battle of Fredericksburg

May 1–6, 1863	Battle of Chancellorsville
May 10, 1863	Confederate General Thomas "Stonewall" Jackson dies
May 18–July 4, 1863	Battle of Vicksburg
July 1–3, 1863	Battle of Gettysburg
July 18, 1863	Battle of Fort Wagner
September 2, 1864	Union army captures Atlanta, Georgia
November 15–December 21, 1864	General Sherman's march to the sea
April 2, 1865	Union army captures Petersburg, Virginia
April 9, 1865	General Lee surrenders to General Grant
April 14, 1865	President Lincoln is shot at Ford's Theatre and dies the next day
May 26, 1865	Confederates' final surrender
December 6, 1865	States ratify the 13th Amendment abolishing slavery

Glossary

abolitionist during the Civil War period, a person who wanted to end slavery in the United States

aide assistant to a military officer

amputate remove a limb in a medical procedure

artillery cannons, and the soldiers who fire them

battery group of cannons in one location

bayonet steel knife attached to the end of a rifle that is used in hand-to-hand combat

bluff steep cliff

bow front end of a ship

brigade large unit of ground troops

cavalry soldiers who fight on horseback

civilian any person who is not in active duty in the military

Emancipation Proclamation document issued by President Lincoln that granted freedom to slaves living in Confederate states when those states did not return to the Union by January 1, 1863

engagement any conflict between opposing military forces

federal related to a central or national government, as opposed to the governments of individual states

flank far right or left side of a military formation

Gettysburg Address speech given by President Lincoln when part of the Gettysburg battlefield was dedicated as a cemetery

harvest gather or collect a crop when it is ready

hull body or frame of a ship

infantry soldiers who fight on foot, typically using rifles

ironclad warship covered with iron plates

manufacturing making or producing things to sell

Overland Campaign General Grant's six-week movement and fighting through Virginia during the spring of 1864; his goal was to capture Richmond, the Confederate capital

plantation large farm or estate that is worked by a large number of laborers, like slaves

pontoon boat or other floating structure; wood planks are laid on the pontoons to build a temporary bridge

prejudice holding negative feelings or opinions toward a person or group of people based on race, religion, or nationality

ram heavy metal beam attached to the front of a warship used to pierce the side of an enemy ship

ratify approve

Rebel Confederate supporter

regiment military unit of foot soldiers

reinforcements additional troops that come to support an army

secede break away from something

sharpshooter person skilled in shooting a gun, especially a rifle

siege military strategy of surrounding a city and cutting it off from support and supplies in order to force it to surrender

surrender quit a battle, admitting defeat

trench long, deep ditch that serves as protection in battle

turret small iron-plated tower on top of a warship; weapons are mounted within the turret, which can turn in any direction

waterway river or other body of water used for shipping or transportation

Yankee Union supporter

Find Out More

Books

Abnett, Dan. *The Battle of Gettysburg: Spilled Blood on Sacred Ground*. Graphic Battles of the Civil War series. New York: Rosen Publishing Group, 2007.

Abnett, Dan. *The* Monitor *vs. the* Merrimac*: Ironclads at War!* Graphic Battles of the Civil War series. New York: Rosen Publishing Group, 2007.

Hama, Larry. *The Battle of Antietam: The Bloodiest Day of Battle*. Graphic Battles of the Civil War series. New York: Rosen Publishing Group, 2007.

Hama, Larry. *The Battle of Shiloh: Surprise Attack!* Graphic Battles of the Civil War series. New York: Rosen Publishing Group, 2007.

O'Muir, G. *Causes and Effects of the Civil War*. New York: PowerKids Press, 2009.

Websites

http://eyewitnesstohistory.com/
Click on the links to find out more about the different battles and to read accounts from people who were alive at the time of the events.

http://socialstudiesforkids.com/subjects/civilwarbattles.htm
This website contains a timeline, a glossary, maps, and much more information related to the battles of the Civil War.

DVDs

The History Channel Presents The Civil War (DVD) (1999). History Channel DVDs, 2007.

Index

13th Amendment 43

54th Massachusetts Infantry 38–39

abolitionists 5, 38

African-American soldiers 38–39

Appomattox Court House, Virginia 43

Army of Northern Virginia 7, 23, 28, 34

Army of Tennessee 7

Army of the Potomac 7, 26, 28, 34

Army of the Tennessee 17, 31

artillery 26, 30

Baltimore and Ohio Railroad 23

Battle of Antietam 22–23, 24

Battle of Bull Run (First) 10–11, 12, 13

Battle of Bull Run (Second) 20–21

Battle of Chancellorsville 28–29

Battle of Fort Wagner 39

Battle of Fredericksburg 26–27

Battle of Gettysburg 34, 35, 36–37

Battle of Shiloh 17–18

Battle of the Wilderness 42

Battle of Vicksburg 30, 31–33, 37

Beauregard, Pierre G. T. 11

Bee, Barnard 12

Bloody Lane 24

Burnside, Ambrose 24, 26, 28

Carney, William H. 39

Cemetery Ridge 35

Confederate States of America 6, 8, 9, 14, 22, 25, 26, 29, 32, 42

Congressional Medal of Honor 39

CSS Virginia 14, 15

Davis, Jefferson 6, 9

deaths 7, 8, 9, 12, 18, 21, 24, 27, 29, 35, 37, 39, 43

deserters 13

Douglass, Frederick 38

economies 4–5

Emancipation Proclamation 25, 38

Fort Donelson 17

Fort Henry 17

Fort Sumter 8–9, 41

Fort Wagner 39

Gettysburg Address 36

Grant, Ulysses S. 17, 18, 31, 32, 33, 40, 42, 43

Greenhow, Rose O'Neal 11

Hooker, Joseph 28, 29

Hornet's Nest 18, 19

ironclads 14, 15, 16, 31

Jackson, Thomas "Stonewall" 12, 20, 23, 29

Johnston, Albert Sidney 18

Johnston, Joseph E. 12, 40

Lee, Robert E. 20, 21, 22–23, 26, 28, 29, 34, 36, 42, 43

Lincoln, Abraham 4, 6, 9, 10, 25, 28, 30, 36, 43

Longstreet, James 20, 21

maps 4, 6, 8, 23, 32, 34, 37, 41

"march to the sea" 41

McClellan, George 20, 23, 24, 26

McDowell, Irvin 10, 11

Meade, George 35

Mississippi River 30, 31, 32, 33

Overland Campaign 42

Pemberton, John C. 33

Pickett, George 36

Pickett's Charge 36, 37

plantations 5

pontoon bridges 26

Pope, John 20, 21

railroads 10, 11, 17, 23, 41

Reconstruction 43

retreat 12, 18, 24, 27, 29, 31, 37

secession 6, 8

Shaw, Robert Gould 38, 39

Sherman, William 40–41

slavery 5, 6, 25, 38, 43

spies 11

states' rights 5

Sumter, Thomas 9

supplies 9, 10, 14, 17, 26, 30, 31, 33, 34, 37, 40

surrender 8, 15, 18, 33, 43

uniforms 9, 12

USS Congress 15

USS Merrimac 14

USS Monitor 16

weapons 8, 9, 10, 15, 16, 26, 30, 36, 43